THE JESUS OVER YOURSELF® DEVOTIONAL WORKBOOK

CHOOSE JOY
Jesus Over Yourself

A Jumpstart To Your **Healing Journey** of Choosing
Jesus Over Your Feelings, Fears, Frustrations, and Flesh

JACLYN SMALL

Copyright © 2018 Jaclyn Small

www.JaclynSmall.com
www.JesusOverYourself.com

All rights reserved. No portion of this publication may be reproduced, stored in a retrieval system, or transmitted in any form or by any means—electronic, mechanical, photocopy, recording, or any other—except for brief quotations in printed reviews, without the prior permission of the copyright owner.

ISBN-13: 978-1-7320660-0-7

Scripture quotations taken from the Amplified® Bible (AMP),
Copyright © 2015 by The Lockman Foundation
Used by permission. www.Lockman.org

Scripture quotations taken from the New American Standard Bible® (NASB),
Copyright © 1960, 1962, 1963, 1968,1971, 1972, 1973, 1975,
1977, 1995 by The Lockman Foundation
Used by permission. www.Lockman.org

Scripture quotations taken from the New King James Version®. Copyright © 1982 by Thomas Nelson. Used by permission. All rights reserved.

Scriptures taken from the Holy Bible, New International Version®, NIV®. Copyright © 1973, 1978, 1984, 2011 by Biblica, Inc.™ Used by permission of Zondervan. All rights reserved worldwide. www.zondervan.com The "NIV" and "New International Version" are trademarks registered in the United States Patent and Trademark Office by Biblica, Inc.™

Scripture quotations marked (NLT) are taken from the Holy Bible, New Living Translation, copyright ©1996, 2004, 2015 by Tyndale House Foundation. Used by permission of Tyndale House Publishers, Inc., Carol Stream, Illinois 60188. All rights reserved.

Written by Jaclyn Small

Edited by Natasha Herring

Dedicated to my amazing husband.

You are the example of a husband who lives out Ephesians 5:25. Thank you for continually loving me as Christ loves the church, and choosing Jesus Over Yourself. I love you handsome!

Table of Contents

INTRODUCTION 1

IDENTIFY BONDAGE **5**
WALK IT OUT 9

HEART CHECK **13**
WALK IT OUT 17

MIND CHECK **23**
WALK IT OUT 29

BELIEF SYSTEM **33**
WALK IT OUT 37

UPROOT LIES **40**
WALK IT OUT 48

RECITE TRUTH **55**
WALK IT OUT 59

CHOOSE J.O.Y. **61**
WALK IT OUT 63

Introduction

"Come close to God [with a contrite heart] and He will come close to you." – James 4:8

The **Jesus Over Yourself® (J.O.Y.) Movement** was birthed from a place of being stuck. I served a sovereign God, but I was stuck in the same cycles, same struggles, same strongholds, same fears and I was **TIRED** of it. How could I possibly be a daughter of the King, the one who sets captives free, and still feel...bound?

Don't get me wrong, God had done a transformation in my life! In college, I was a Division I basketball player, who was a hot mess; I cussed every other word, was "confident" on the outside, but insecure on the inside, and perfectionist who was seeking affirmation from others. When I received Jesus as my Lord and Savior, I had a radical transformation, and I was on fire for the Lord, growing in my walk, seeking His face, His will and His plan. However, years into my walk I still struggled with foundational issues that caused my feelings, fears, and frustrations to lead me, rather than the Holy Spirit. I was growing in Christ and moving in and out of life stages, all while still struggling in certain areas.

INTRODUCTION

No matter how hard I tried to act right and be right, there was no true *transformation*, until the Lord provided revelation. The J.O.Y. Movement was conceived from my own life transformation where God freed me from being led by my feelings, fears, frustrations, and flesh. Jesus Over Yourself® exists to equip the bride of Christ for the present war, and the coming wedding. But it started as a movement to encourage and equip women to choose Jesus every day, and this workbook was born out of it. Maybe you can relate to my story of walking with God but feeling stuck, *or* maybe you're strenghtening an already firm foundation in Christ and recognize the need for healing in certain areas– either way, I believe God will use this devotional to transform your life.

This devotional workbook is your jumpstart to choosing Jesus Over Yourself®. It will prompt you to begin the deep heart work of identifying strongholds and re-aligning your life against God's truth, day by day and thought by thought. Each part includes a section to "Walk It Out," this is your chance to apply what you've learned in your life. Often, we think transformation happens in a moment like salvation; however, transformation takes us intentionally applying God's Word to our life. I challenge you to commit **NOW** to your transformation process and to walking in freedom. This devotional gives you a blueprint for how to stop living captive to your feelings and begin living an abundant life led by the Holy Spirit.

I've included seven foundational principles in the journey of choosing Jesus Over Yourself®. This devotional workbook is designed to be completed with the Holy Spirit, at the pace He leads you. If the Holy Spirit stops you on forgiveness, remain there and let Him work fully in you! It is also often repeated in it's entirety more than once, as the Lord often peels back layers of healing as we go. This is the beauty of becoming more like Him. The material is simple enough to digest yet impactful so the Word of God becomes rooted into your spirit, your thought process, your will, and your emotions. The purpose of this workbook and my prayer for you is that choosing Jesus Over Yourself® becomes your new normal.

The Lord showed me a short, simple, devotional that would bring to life the very principles needed to start you on your journey of moving you past your feelings, fears, frustrations and flesh. But ultimately, the choice is yours. Inspired by James 1:22-25, this workbook is meant to be put into action, not just ingested. Let's prove ourselves doers of the Word, and not merely listeners— because when we do, according to Scripture (below), we will be blessed and favored by God in what we do.

22 But prove yourselves doers of the word [actively and continually obeying God's precepts], and not merely listeners [who hear the word but fail to internalize its meaning], deluding yourselves [by unsound reasoning contrary to the truth].
23 For if anyone only listens to the word without obeying it, he is like a man who looks very carefully at his natural face in a mirror;

INTRODUCTION

24 for once he has looked at himself and gone away, he immediately forgets what he looked like.
25 But he who looks carefully into the perfect law, the law of liberty, and faithfully abides by it, not having become a [careless] listener who forgets but an active doer [who obeys], he will be blessed and favored by God in what he does [in his life of obedience].
- James 1:22-25 AMP

He is with you, He is for you. Journey through this with Him!

- *Jaclyn Small*

IDENTIFY BONDAGE

"The thief does not come except to steal, and to kill, and to destroy. ***I have come that they may have life, and that they may have it more abundantly****. "I am the good shepherd. The good shepherd gives His life for the sheep."*
- John 10:10-11 (NKJV)

The objective of the thief, Satan, is the direct opposite of that of Jesus. Satan comes only to steal and to kill and to destroy. Let's make one thing clear: Jesus came so that we would have *abundant life*. It's not complicated. Anything that isn't in line with abundant life is residual from the influence from Satan, the fall, and sin. Too many of us are unaware that we are lingering in Satan's ploys.

In my own ignorance, I was living this out! With a hopeful but unsure heart, I prayed, studied, worshipped, yet remained bound, because I lacked knowledge. Hosea 4:6 says that "My people are destroyed for lack of knowledge [of My law, where I reveal My will]." I kept wondering if I would ever truly be free from the bondage and

ONE

old ways of thinking that I lived with. I kept crying out to God for freedom, but I wasn't sure if it was God's will.

For far too long, I was not positioned to wage war on the attacks on my life, because I was unclear if God kept allowing this for a specific purpose. Although He used the attacks, it wasn't His will, which we find in His Word. At some point, you may have thrown up your hands and lost hope thinking, *this* is all life will ever be because God hasn't healed you, freed you, or delivered you. You may be caught in a destructive cycle emotionally and relationally – believing that you can't break free and that God doesn't have more for you. *This is a lie*. It doesn't line up with Scripture. Bondage is not the abundant life that Jesus came to give you.

The Truth About Suffering

Have you ever prayed for God's will to be done on earth as it is in heaven? I know I have many times. When we try earnestly to get free from bondage, but our efforts are unsuccessful or short-lived, we accept and justify our struggles as a part of God's will. When this happens, the miracles, healings, and freedom we read about in the Bible or see across the globe *seem* out of reach or even impossible. Your bondage is NOT God's will! Let this serve as a reminder to never let your experiences have a stronger influence on what God's will entails for you than the Word of God.

We cannot afford to confuse persecution (suffering for the sake of the gospel) with disease, sickness, or torment as some sort of God-ordained method of making us more like Christ. Hosea 4:6 says "My people are destroyed for lack of knowledge." Bondage, sickness, disease, poverty, are not part of God's design for our life.

ONE

We often think that God could be using our strongholds to teach us a lesson, otherwise why would He allow us to endure it? But it's important to remember that while Jesus came to give us *abundant life*, Satan is actively trying steal, kill, and destroy that very life that Jesus freely offered. We can't *exchange the truth of God for a lie* (Romans 1:25) and expect to experience His freedom! You must realize that Satan is coming for your peace, your joy, your confidence in God, your faith in God, your sound mind, your love, your patience, your goodness, etc. Let's get clear – you CAN walk in authority over bondage, strongholds, lies, attacks, destructive thinking, unhealthy emotions, and so on, because Jesus paid for it on the cross with *His* blood. In fact, when you begin to understand your position in the family of God, you will realize that authority is in your new bloodline.

WALK IT OUT

With that in mind, think of three areas in your life that you have remained bound. Is it your thought life? Are you constantly living with a victim mentality? Is it your marriage? Are you struggling to respect your husband? Are you trying to control everything and everyone around you? Are you bound by people's opinions? Is fear driving you? Are you constantly looking for affirmation from men, women, coworkers, peers and others, instead of walking soundly in who God created you to be? List three areas that you've been bound in:

1 _____

2 _____

3 _____

ONE

For each area of bondage you listed on page 9, describe how it impacts your life, and how it plays out in the day to day when Satan has his way and the door is open to him in these areas. Then on the next page, write what it would look like if each of those areas of bondage was completely surrendered to and healed by Jesus.

SATAN - Gratification of the flesh, jealousy, manipulation, idolatry, divisions, destruction, riddled with fear, etc.

1. _____
   _____
   _____

2. _____
   _____
   _____

3. _____
   _____

JESUS - Abounding in the fruit of the Spirit, full of love, power, and a sound mind. (*Galatians 5:22-23*)

Example: "I would no longer fear, or manipulate!" "My heart would be..."

1. _____
   _____
   _____
   _____

2. _____
   _____
   _____
   _____

3. _____
   _____
   _____
   _____

ONE

Throughout the rest of the workbook, these descriptions will help you to identify whose voice you're listening to and whose plan you're operating under. You will recognize which areas of your heart, mind, and life the devil has a hold on. You can believe in Jesus but still align with Satan's plan unknowingly— that's why he is called a liar and a deceiver.

Identifying the difference doesn't mean we've solved the problem, but that we will be equipped to stand on the solid foundation, Scripture, when the enemy has crept in. By doing this work with the Holy Spirit, you are exposing the enemy's work in your life, coming out of agreement with it, and coming into agreement with the Lord Jesus Christ!

Two

HEART CHECK

8 The one who practices sin [separating himself from God, and offending Him by acts of disobedience, indifference, or rebellion] is of the devil [and takes his inner character and moral values from him, not God]; for the devil has sinned and violated God's law from the beginning. **The Son of God appeared for this purpose, to destroy the works of the devil.**

9 No one who is **born of God** *[deliberately, knowingly, and habitually] practices sin, because God's seed [His principle of life, the essence of His righteous character] remains [permanently] in him [who is born again—who is reborn from above—spiritually transformed, renewed, and set apart for His purpose]; and he [who is born again] cannot habitually [live a life characterized by] sin, because he is born of God and longs to please Him.*
-1 John 3:8-9 (AMP)

I want to focus on the two bolded parts of verse 8 and 9, but first, let's clarify these verses don't mean that if you sin, you are of

TWO

the devil. The apostle John is referring to those who willfully and deliberately employ themselves to sin without repentance. No one, believers included, lives a sinless life; we are born into sin and wage war against it daily.

The Son of God appeared for this purpose, to destroy the works of the devil.

Jesus' purpose was to destroy the works of the devil; the work of the devil is to tempt people to sin. When we sin, the devil's work is accomplished. Because you struggle with a sin or can't seem to do right, doesn't mean that Jesus' work on the cross doesn't apply to you. But the Scripture says that Jesus appeared for the very purpose of destroying sin. What it means is that the birth, life, death, burial, and resurrection of Jesus Christ broke the power of sin.

"And because you belong to him, the power of the life-giving Spirit has freed you from the power of sin that leads to death."
– Romans 8:2 (NLT)

Born of God...

Jesus' work on the cross didn't end our ability to sin, rather it freed believers from the power of sin that previously had control over us. When you are a believer in Jesus Christ, you are born of

God, or reborn into His family, and in His family, the dominion of sin is destroyed. Walking in the newness of who you are in Christ doesn't mean that you are sinless. It means that you desire to see your sin the way God sees your sin, and you come into agreement with Him regarding it. This is the key: When we begin to see sin the way God sees sin, we are led to repentance.

Seeing It How God's Sees It

Here's an example that maybe you can relate to. My life had programmed me to protect and defend myself at all costs, even if that meant disrespecting others depending on how they responded to me. When I got married, my mindset came with me; it didn't magically change overnight. So when I didn't get my way with my husband or if he disagreed with me, I would respond disrespectfully. I failed repeatedly at respecting him; it was an ugly, sin-filled, destructive cycle. What frustrated me most was feeling like I couldn't break the cycle. I was a redeemed, saved, and sanctified believer, who wanted to pray the cycle away and still *get my way.* I tried praying, journaling, counseling. All of those were helpful, but real change came when I truly asked God to reveal the root of this frustrating cycle. God showed me that I wanted to respect my husband because God's Word told me to (law), not because my heart wanted what God wanted (love). When I started to see my sin the way God saw my sin, I was led to repentance and God's love touched my heart. From my new heart posture, I no

TWO

longer wanted my actions to line up with the Word of God, but I wanted the Word to motivate my actions. It's no surprise God mentioned, "Guard your heart above all else, for it determines the course of your life." (Proverbs 4:23 NLT).

WALK IT OUT

Now that you know sin does not have control over you, you need to identify WHY it's still controlling you. For the three areas you identified in part one, write down how you live it out. Does the way you live or view it agree with how God views it? For instance, I knew logically that I should respect my husband, but every time I gave my husband attitude, it revealed that I truly didn't agree with God's view in my heart. Our actions reveal our heart's affections. Whatever comes out of your mouth reveals what is truly in your heart. What's coming out of your mouth?

"The good man out of the good treasure of his heart brings forth what is good; and the evil man out of the evil treasure brings forth what is evil; for his mouth speaks from that which fills his heart."
- Luke 6:45 (NASB)

For your three areas, write how you view it. Share how this area operates in your heart, mind, will and emotions on a daily basis.

TWO

My View:

1

2

THE JESUS OVER YOURSELF® DEVOTIONAL WORKBOOK

3
_____
_____
_____
_____
_____
_____

Now compare your heart to God's heart (Scripture) concerning those areas. Search the Scriptures regarding your areas to uncover what God says about it.

God's View:

1
_____
_____
_____
_____
_____
_____

TWO

2

3

Where does your view and God's view disagree? That's where your work lies.

Three

MIND CHECK

"So if the Son makes you free, then you are unquestionably free." - John 8:36 (AMP)

This verse used to really frustrate me. When life was going well, I felt free. When life was bad, I crashed hard back into bondage, wondering if I would ever break free again. It was a rollercoaster that too easily shifted from well to bondage. I would confess that I was free, but I still felt bound. *I still felt stuck.* No matter what I did, I couldn't shake the thought that I had to *prove my value* in order to be loved; I was just *not good enough.* I was in a cycle of needing to control everything in order to prove my worth and value; I would constantly replay situations in my mind and critique myself with a list of "shoulda, coulda, wouldas." The verse says, "the Son set me free?" But I knew this was NOT freedom.

I tried many remedies.
I *journaled.* I *prayed.*
I *studied* the Word of God.

THREE

I worshipped. I served.

I went to *Christian counseling*, where I processed my deeply rooted issues, and together we addressed every last one of them. This process revealed that I had a rejection mindset linked to my father who abandoned my family when I was young; I did the *work* and forgave him. I learned from two ex-boyfriends who cheated that I needed to prove I was worthy of love; I did the work and forgave them. While growing up, the mistreatment from authority figures resulted in a fear-based portrayal of perfectionism for all authority, even church authority. Again, I did the work and forgave them. I *forgave* others and myself.

Forgiveness

Forgiveness is paramount. Your healing, freedom, and ability to grow will only go as far as your willingness to forgive others. If you hold unforgiveness in your heart toward anyone you will continue to face the same issues.

Forgiveness is a vertical process between you and God. It does not require an apology from someone, nor does it require a conversation with them, but it does require you to confront your hurts and let God make you whole. Tangibly, this may look like writing a ten-page letter to release everything you've held in, only to burn it up after!

In some cases, you may get the opportunity to speak with the person that hurt you. If so, remember that forgiveness has nothing to do with the other person's response; ultimately, forgiveness is between you and the Lord. After all, Jesus didn't wait until we repented to die for us. He did it while we were still sinners, based on who He is and His love for us. Now we have the choice to forgive others based on the fact that we, too, are forgiven. When you fully grasp the weight of His forgiveness toward you, you can make the choice to extend it to others.

Your Freedom is in Your Forgiveness

The result of forgiveness is that you have released the power that your offender had over you and they no longer owe you anything.

Your unforgiveness only hurts you. Your forgiveness only frees you.

Here's how to start: Write a list of people that you need to forgive. Identify what they did to hurt you and how that's impacted your life. Pray and declare over every person that you forgive them for what they did. Release them from the debt they owe you. Pray that God will heal your wounds and lead you into wholeness in every impacted area.

I *spoke*. In fact, in 2010, I taught women how to get to the root of their issues. I would illustrate by using the example of a tree that has rotten fruit— let's say cussing is the rotten fruit. You cannot expect that picking off all the rotten fruit would make the tree healthy. If you pick off all the rotten fruit, the tree will produce more *rotten* fruit. In the same way, you cannot expect to just stop cussing; eventually, when you're put in the right (or wrong) situation, cuss words will flow out. **In order to change to fruit, you need to address the root.**

To summarize, my efforts healed specific wounds from each situation, but my belief system and patterns of thinking remained the same. My mind was still operating on defense mechanisms and unhealthy ways of thinking. Like me, your soul wounds could be healed, but your mind may not be transformed. **We need healing and transformation.**

And do not be conformed to this world [any longer with its superficial values and customs], but
be [a]transformed and progressively changed [as you mature spiritually] by the renewing of your mind [focusing on godly values and ethical attitudes], so that you may prove [for yourselves] what the will of God is, that which is good and acceptable and perfect [in His plan and purpose for you].
- Romans 12:2 (AMP)

THREE

John 8:36 says, "you are truly free." It is completely up to you to receive and walk in your freedom. You will not only see your wounds healed, but also have your mind renewed with the Word of God. The promise is *already* granted. As a daughter of the Most High God, you have authority to believe and act on God's promises. Often, we expect that God's wisdom for our lives will meet us on our doorstep right when we expect it, like an Amazon package we ordered. If we're honest, we may see glimpses of the freedom we have in Christ from social media, but we scroll past them, choosing to be entertained and remain passive. Sister, this is your wake-up call. You can read the Scripture all day, post encouraging verses, confide in trustworthy friends, preach the Word of God, but until you renew your mind, *transformation* is not possible. Get up, sister. Our Father's promises await you.

WALK IT OUT

What new or old wounds are you walking around with that have been left unhealed?

_____
_____
_____
_____
_____
_____
_____
_____
_____
_____
_____

THREE

How will you actively confront those wounds? (Christian counseling, forgiveness, etc.)

What thoughts and actions have developed as a result of those wounds?

THREE

In what ways does your mind need to be transformed?

Four

YOUR BELIEF SYSTEM

WHATEVER YOU FEED, GROWS.

Lies are like seeds and if you water them, they grow. There are lies associated with soul wounds from your past that the enemy wants to let fester. For instance, if your father left when you were a child, you probably adopted a lie that you had to work for love or you weren't worthy of love. If you agree with those lies, they take root and become an open door for Satan in your life. With each lie that you believe, your personality, thought-life, and mindset will shift to center around the lie. Over time, these rehearsed lies become strongholds— incorrect thinking patterns in your mind that affect your actions and worldview.

Lies can be whatever you believe about yourself as a result of a soul wound. Every wound caused by others is an opportunity for Satan to lie to you. If he can, he will start to use wound after wound to reinforce the original lie he planted. This way, he doesn't even have to keep working at it. He reinforces the same lie so that it

FOUR

gets rooted more deeply until you are completely bound by it. This is when you begin operating on autopilot under the lies that you've believed about who you are. By the time you decide to heal from that wound, you've already adopted a lie about your identity based on many wounds; it's a destructive cycle. As a result, you may create false scenarios in your head that aren't true. For instance, you think people are rejecting you when they are not, or you believe someone is hating on you, when they are not. Your perceptions are out of alignment with God's truth.

If you believe a lie, you will live a lie. Your identity is shaped around what you believe. In order to heal you have to be aware of what thoughts you are entertaining and magnifying. Whatever you focus on will grow. If you constantly rehearse that you aren't enough, you will live in agreement with that statement. That's what the Word means when it says, "death and life are in the power of the tongue."

"Death and life are in the power of the tongue, and those who love it and indulge it will eat its fruit and bear the consequences of their words." - Proverbs 18:21 (AMP)

This isn't some mysteriously magical verse that means we create something out of nothing from our words. It simply means that what we confess out of our mouths we begin to embed in our spirit. Our confession becomes our belief. The Message translation puts it plainly, "words kill, words give life; they're either poison or fruit—you choose." Your words, as mentioned previously, will tell you what is in your heart. If you aren't sure about what lies you've believed, listen to the words you speak every day. Since *out of the abundance of the heart the mouth speaks*, you can count on your mouth to reveal what is going on inside of you.

My first job out of college was at ESPN; well, it was my first *official* job. I remember wanting to leave everything in my past behind me and start afresh living the life I wanted to live. I was in a new state, with a new job, new wardrobe, and new friends. Unfortunately, my deeply rooted habits tainted my fresh new life with my past. This is where my serious work on my belief system started.

You have to reexamine your belief system and set it up against what the Word of God says. You have to challenge, change, and correct what you've believed to make it align with what God's Word says about you. *What is normal to you may actually be unhealthy.* Just because something is familiar and comfortable doesn't mean it's healthy or God's best for your life. Whatever lies you've believed, it's time to dethrone them.

It's your responsibility to examine and till the soil in your own garden. This means you must ask the tough questions and continue to uproot the lies that have taken root in the garden of your mind. This isn't easy. It's much easier to believe a lie than dig

FOUR

for the truth. But, this is the necessary soul work that leads to walking in the freedom that is already available to you.

WALK IT OUT

What wounds, hurts, attacks, and/or abuses have you experienced?

_____
_____
_____
_____
_____
_____
_____
_____
_____
_____
_____
_____
_____

FOUR

What lies were planted in your mind as a result of those wounds?

How have your words and actions reinforced those lies over the years?

FOUR

In what ways do those lies manifest in your life today? (defensive, anxious, in relationships etc.)?

___

Five

UPROOT THE LIES

Now that you've identified lies you've been believing and internalizing, it's time to uproot them from the soil of your heart. Uprooting these lies starts with challenging them with the truth. Weeds grow in a garden just like flowers; as you till your garden, you uproot the weeds so that they don't choke out the flowers. We have to do the same with our thoughts.

We uproot lies one by one by gathering evidence of God's truth about each lie we've believed. For instance, if you believe the lie that you aren't loved, search the Scriptures for what God's Word says about you being loved. You will find that God *rejoices* over you with singing and that He loves you with an *everlasting* love. The truth is that He loved you so much that He sent His Son to die on the cross for you. In fact, even before the foundations of the earth, He knew you. He created your innermost being in the womb—everything about you He intended and created fearfully and wonderfully. This is what you will discover is true. Each lie that was deeply rooted inside of you from a painful experience needs to be challenged with the God's truth.

> *"We are destroying sophisticated arguments and every exalted and proud thing that sets itself up against the [true] knowledge of God, and we are taking every thought and purpose captive to the obedience of Christ."*
> - 2 Corinthians 10:5 (AMP)

We must uproot these lies one by one by comparing our thoughts against what the Word says. For every thought that doesn't agree with the Word, we take it captive and make that thought obey Christ, the Living Word. When we do not take thoughts captive and cast them down, we allow them to build strongholds in us. Each time you own a thought and don't cast it down, you give it room to rule. We have to stop owning thoughts of rejection, depression, anxiety, worthlessness, etc., and start owning the God's truth about it. We cannot afford to have thoughts about ourselves that God does not have about us. It is our choice to take those untrue thoughts captive and replace them with truth.

Going Deeper

To go deeper, we need to actively replace lies with the truth. The practical steps to replace a *lie* with the *truth* include:

    A) Find Scriptures that prove the untrue thought to be a lie.
    B) Make the Scripture personal.
    C) Pray the personal Scripture out loud.
    D) Declare the Scriptural based affirmation over yourself. See the example below.

Lie

I am unlovable. No one loves me. I am not worthy of being loved.

Truth
(based on Scripture)

- Even if people's "love" didn't last, your love for me is everlasting Abba Father! (Jeremiah 31:3)
- Even if my own mother or father didn't love me, You love me, and You always will. I belong to You. You've literally written my name on the palms of Your hands. (Isaiah 49: 15-16)
- It doesn't matter what is going on around me, Your love for me will not be shaken. Nothing can change it. Even as the years pass and the world changes, Your love is faithful, and it remains. Period. (Isaiah 54:10)
- Nothing can separate me from Your love. Nothing I did. Nothing I will do. Nothing someone else did. You love me with an inseparable love. (Romans 8:35)
- Lord, You love me so much that You laid down Your life for me. (John 15:13)

FIVE

Captive literally means held under the control of another or owned or controlled by another. In this case, we take the thought captive and bring it under submission to Jesus Christ, the truth. So, we come out of agreement with the lie, meaning it no longer runs free in our minds; the lie becomes a prisoner to Jesus and it must obey what is true. The lie can no longer take root and grow in our mind; it can no longer run free in our temple. It is now held captive, and then it must obey Christ. This is how we come out of agreement with the lies we have unknowingly and unintentionally partnered with.

In order to uproot these lies, you have to know God. You have to know His nature and who He truly is based on His Word. Many of us believe lies about God because our image of God was shaped by the image of our earthly parents or caregivers. For instance, if your father was a perfectionist and you couldn't make a mistake, you may view God as a rule punisher or policing God. With this perspective, you see yourself as needing to be perfect or else.... Or maybe you've dealt with unfair people, so subconsciously you think God is an unjust dictator whom you must fight or bargain with for fair treatment. These are lies. The truth is that **God is a merciful and just God**. He isn't expecting perfection, nor is He disappointed in you.

Whether we like it or not, the way we naturally relate to God is impacted by the very people that we encountered throughout our lives, especially our earthly parents. You may have head knowledge concerning God's nature, but you lack heart knowledge and have a hard time believing that you don't really need to get it right all the time. You *know* being perfect is unrealistic and unreachable, but at the same time you beat yourself up when you aren't perfect. Let's be honest, we've all been there. The areas that weren't fulfilled early in your life will be the same areas you seek to fulfill and may struggle with in your relationship with God. Any false view of God will lead to an unhealthy concept of yourself. Thus, you need to correct your thinking concerning God and align what you believe with what God believes.

Head Knowledge vs. Heart Knowledge

When we know something logically, it acts as insight. This is why we are instructed in Proverbs 3:5 to "Trust in the Lord with all your heart and lean not on your own understanding" because what we understand in the mind is limited to our thoughts and our own comprehension.

Application is an indication of heart knowledge. Living it out reveals that we understand it in our heart, which spurs us to take action. This is wisdom! It shows that we've encountered God and that we believe what He says in His word. This belief requires intimacy with God.

So, it's time to uproot those lies that you've believed. Even the ones that you attached the "that's just who I am" explanation to. Yep, those ones too! One of the first and most critical areas that Satan attacks is your identity, because if your identity is not in Christ, it will cause your soul and relationships to be unstable. When your identity is rooted in lies, you cannot possibly walk in freedom or fulfill what God has called you to do.

FIVE

WALK IT OUT

If you do not have the mind of Christ, what or who has your mind?

_____

_____

_____

_____

_____

_____

_____

You are going to combat each lie that you wrote yesterday with a truth from the Word. If you aren't sure where to start, categorize the lie (marriage, relationships, God's love, anxiety, fear), and then search the Scriptures to uncover what the Bible says regarding that topic. Next to "LIE" you will write what you have believed about yourself as a result of someone else's treatment towards you. Then next to "TRUTH" you will write what Scripture says about it.

LIE

TRUTH

LIE

FIVE

TRUTH ———

LIE ———

TRUTH ———

LIE

TRUTH

LIE

FIVE

TRUTH _____

LIE _____

TRUTH _____

LIE

TRUTH

Six

RECITE THE TRUTH

"For as he thinketh in his heart, so is he..."
- Proverbs 23:7 NKJV

I needed to know the truth or remember Scripture, so I was writing verses out on note cards, using an app on my phone to memorize them, journaling, and everything else. The more verses I learned, the more frustrated I became, because I was not seeing the transformation I expected. I remember asking the Lord, "What else can I do?"

I had great moments where I truly experienced Jesus and was freed from certain things from my past, but the lingering strongholds and struggles seemed to remain in spite of how many verses I learned. I kept pressing into the Word and journaling, but again, I felt like freedom was far away. I even started speaking Scripture out loud, because I know that Satan is the prince of the power of the air (Ephesians 2:2) and I needed to start addressing him directly! But something was still missing.

Dig Deeper

In Ephesians 2:2, Satan is referred to as the "prince of the power of the air" which tells us a few things.

- We must recognize that although Satan has power, he does not have authority—unless you allow him to walk in *your* authority.
- Satan is referred to as a "prince" because he has a kingdom (Matthew 12:26) and a throne (Revelation 2:13) where he rules and possesses power to command demons to carry out evil. More importantly, he is called a prince because there is only one King with all power, his name is Jesus.
- The "air" represents the spiritual realm where Satan holds power. If we are ignorant or not walking in our authority, the demons that are assigned to our lives will cloud our thinking, distort our judgment, and ultimately use our God-given authority for evil.

⁹ If you declare with your mouth, "Jesus is Lord," and believe in your heart that God raised him from the dead, you will be saved. ¹⁰ For it is with your heart that you believe and are justified, and it is with your mouth that you profess your faith and are saved. - Romans 10:9-10 (NIV)

Many of us are walking around confessing that Jesus is Lord, declaring that we are chosen children of God, claiming our victory, and even reminding Satan that we have authority, but yet, **we are not experiencing the realities associated with all of those truths.** If we break down verses 9 and 10 we find two things:

1. Confess with your mouth: this means to declare or make something known by speaking it

2. Believe in your heart: Believing something in your heart indicates that you consider it to be truth; it becomes a rooted opinion of yours.

A lot of us have the first part covered— confessing with our mouths, but we don't actually **believe** it in our hearts. We know logically that we are adopted into God's family as daughters, but we don't accept it as truth because we've been conditioned by a lie for so long. So, now that you've identified what those lies are, uprooted them, and established the truth against those lies, it's time to

SIX

confess the truth and believe it in your heart. Whatever you believe in your heart is what you become— and if you believe lies, you can't receive the truth you are speaking aloud.

First, take lies captive and uproot them. Second, confess God's truth and believe it in your heart. Order matters. Otherwise, we are sprinkling truth on the surface of deeply planted lies and expecting change, while receiving disappointment.

Now that you've uprooted the lies and are continually taking thoughts captive so that they can't remain planted, it's time to recite the truth that you believe. This simply means to recite God's Word aloud in a formal manner, or to train or make proficient (masterful) by rehearsal (told again and again). Even if you don't fully believe the truth yet, recite it. You are tilling the soil of your mind for planting. Romans 10:17 tells us that faith comes from hearing, and hearing through the Word of God. Your faith (belief and trust) will be built up as you speak the Word and preach it back to yourself!

WALK IT OUT

It's time to saturate yourself with the truths that you wrote out yesterday so that you can begin to recite them as you take every thought captive and make it obey Christ [the living Word]. Write them on index cards, on your phone notepad, make it your lock screen, a standing notepad or decorative plate on a stand in the kitchen. Wherever you choose, the point is to saturate yourself with what is true so that as you uproot the lies, you have truth readily available for those specific lies until they become embedded in your heart! When a lie begins to creep into your mind, recognize it is a lie, cast it down by coming out of agreement with it, and declare what is true. For instance:

Thought:
As you're scrolling online you come across a photo of something that causes a negative thought about yourself to enter your mind.

Capture it:
Stop scrolling. Take the thought captive by not dwelling on it or letting it go further by becoming an owner in your mind. Catch it – and Check it! Do not let it take up territory in your mind!

Make it obey Christ— The Word:
Confess what is true and make the Scripture personal to you!

CHOOSE
JESUS OVER YOURSELF® Every Day

"Yet in all these things we are more than conquerors through Him who loved us." - Romans 8:37 NKJV

The Word of God affirms that the defeated life is not the Christian life when you walk by the Spirit. In Romans 8:37, Paul reminds us that not only will we win in the end when Jesus returns, but that Jesus has enabled us to win **now** in this life. Through His power, we have authority over the enemy and that we are no longer slaves to sin.

Despite all these things that Satan throws at us to destroy us, we win! Despite our sin-nature, we win! Despite our struggles, we win! Overwhelming victory is ours through Christ, who loves us. That victory is present tense. Right now, **you** are more than a conqueror. God desires for you to live in victory...and when you do, He gets the glory. The gospel also affirms that you cannot break free from the sin-cycle in your own strength. You can, however, experience victory over sin by relying on the power of the Holy

SEVEN

Spirit that lives inside of you. The question is, will you choose to submit to your flesh, or to the Spirit?

"But I say, walk habitually in the [Holy] Spirit [seek Him and be responsive to His guidance], and then you will certainly not carry out the desire of the sinful nature [which responds impulsively without regard for God and His precepts]."
- Galatians 5:16 AMP

To habitually do something is to do it over and over and over repeatedly, so much so that it becomes habit. Naturally, your habit is to surrender to your flesh. You resist, but whenever you don't surrender to the Holy Spirit, you automatically surrender to the flesh. Galatians 5:16 says we need to make walking in the Spirit an everyday choice through seeking Him and responding to His guidance. We either choose to respond Jesus or our self. Let's remember the second part of this verse: when you choose Jesus Over Yourself®, you will not carry out the desire of the sinful nature. Every choice of obedience is a step towards freedom and away from bondage. The choice is up to you. The power is yours— every day, every moment, every thought is yours to take captive and submit it to the authority of the Holy Spirit living inside of you. You already have the power of God living inside of you. It's your time to walk in it.

WALK IT OUT

Now it's up to you! It's time to put it into action. Keep taking every thought captive, casting it down, and reciting the truth in its place. As you continue this process of choosing Jesus Over Yourself, you'll notice a pattern of replacing lies with truth and growing closer with Jesus.

Let's review your progress, building off of your work all week. What bondage did you start the week with, what truth have you learned, what truth are choosing to believe and how will you respond in light of your belief?

LIE _____

TRUTH _____

SEVEN

WHAT YOU BELIEVE:

_____
_____
_____
_____
_____
_____
_____

HOW YOU WILL RESPOND:

_____
_____
_____
_____
_____
_____
_____

You may have already experienced a new level of freedom walking in the Spirit regarding these truths that you now believe. **Celebrate** the work you've partnered with God to complete in your life! The habit of replacing God's truth with lies is a *powerful* tool to bring your life in alignment with God.

You may not have experienced progress from the more difficult patterns of thinking. Why does that bondage you've identified in section one still have the same control over you? Meditate and think on your answer to this question.

It's important to remember who you are in Christ, which is why we started with identifying bondage and knowing who God is. Beware not to let a victim mentality, believing *I am not the problem* and *I'm doing the right things*, blind you from dealing directly with your bondage. When you blame others you remain in your current state of bondage. Freedom awaits as you believe what God says about you and surrender to Him. Submitting your heart and mind to Christ means that you allow God to touch your heart. You have the Holy Spirit living on the inside of you; He is your Helper. As you continue going through this process, ask the Holy Spirit to reveal Scriptures to you and clarity on how to navigate your situation.

While this devotional provides practical steps on breaking bondage, it was my revelation from God and intentional work in partnership with the Holy Spirit that did the breaking off of each lie. You cannot do this in your own strength. This is meant to guide you as you surrender to the Holy Spirit and do your part. Many of us

SEVEN

have the faith but aren't putting in the work. This is the work. As you continue on your healing journey, and through this workbook (or certain parts of it) again, intentionally pray and seek God's voice as you reflect and work through each section. Don't move on until you hear from Him. Don't settle for transactional completion, but truly sit with Him.

"Finally, believers, whatever is true, whatever is honorable and worthy of respect, whatever is right and confirmed by God's word, whatever is pure and wholesome, whatever is lovely and brings peace, whatever is admirable and of good repute; if there is any excellence, **if there is anything worthy of praise, think continually on these things [center your mind on them, and implant them in your heart]**. *⁹ The things which you have learned and received and heard and seen in me, practice these things [in daily life], and the God [who is the source] of peace and well-being will be with you."*
- Philippians 4:8-9 (AMP)

We are instructed to think about "these things" that are worthy of praise. Verse 9 states that when we practice these things that the Lord has shown us, the peace of God will be with us. It's about putting it into practice. This is where our choice comes in. We either choose to put His Word into practice or continue practicing our old ways.

THE JESUS OVER YOURSELF® DEVOTIONAL WORKBOOK

Now that you've completed the seven sections, go through and meditate on the pertinent truths again. You've already done the written work, but as you go back, really sit with the Lord concerning the areas He wants to heal you, or the mindset He wants to transform, and seek Him concerning it! Begin to work through the sections that the Holy Spirit is highlighting to you. Maybe it's your thought pattern He is showing you-- go there with Him. Use the blank pages of notes and go deeper. Let Him do the deep work in your soul. Take Him at His word! Whom the Son sets free is free indeed. Seek Him with all your heart until you find Him, and take Him up on His word until it comes to pass!

You have the Spirit of the Living God living in you, and your surrender to Him is your choice to live by His spirit, a life of choosing Jesus Over Yourself®. Walk in the freedom He paid for- it's yours for the taking!

NOTES

Made in United States
Orlando, FL
20 January 2024

42714593R00046